Children's Illustrators

William Steig

Jill C. Wheeler
ABDO Publishing Company

visit us at
www.abdopub.com

Published by ABDO Publishing Company, 4940 Viking Drive, Edina, Minnesota 55435.
Copyright © 2005 by Abdo Consulting Group, Inc. International copyrights reserved in all
countries. No part of this book may be reproduced in any form without written permission from
the publisher. The Checkerboard Library™ is a trademark and logo of ABDO Publishing
Company.

Printed in the United States.

Cover Photo: Getty Images
Interior Photos: AP/Wide World p. 13; Corbis p. 12; Getty Images pp. 5, 7, 8, 9, 10, 11, 14,
    15, 17, 21; HarperCollins p. 19

Series Coordinator: Jennifer R. Krueger
Editors: Stephanie Hedlund, Jennifer R. Krueger
Art Direction: Neil Klinepier

Library of Congress Cataloging-in-Publication Data

Wheeler, Jill C., 1964-
    William Steig / Jill C. Wheeler.
        p. cm. -- (Children's illustrators)
    Includes bibliographical references and index.
    ISBN 1-59197-720-7
    1. Steig, William, 1907---Juvenile literature. 2. Illustrators--United States--Biography--
Juvenile literature. I. Title.

NC975.5.S715W57 2004
741.5'092--dc22
[B]

2004046293

Contents

The Man Who Never Grew Up 4

Dreams of the Sea 6

Family Breadwinner 8

Popular Artist 10

CDB! and the Donkey 12

More Success 16

Creating Colorful Characters 18

Final Chapters 20

Glossary 22

Web Sites 23

Index 24

The Man Who Never Grew Up

William Steig was one of the most famous and talented illustrators of the 1900s. He could also be called one of the busiest. His drawings appeared in the *New Yorker* magazine for more than 70 years. He also wrote more than 30 books for children.

Steig is perhaps best known for writing *Shrek!*, *Sylvester and the Magic Pebble*, and *Doctor De Soto*. Like his other works, these books combine imaginative cartoons with engaging stories. Some show the world through the eyes of a young person. In fact, Steig once said he never felt grown-up.

Steig spent much of his life creating cartoons and books. Sometimes he worked 12 hours a day. Other times he only worked two. He was still drawing in his 90s. He said he felt lucky to have spent his life doing something he really loved.

Opposite Page: *In addition to illustrating, Steig also colored his books with unique phrases that readers love, such as "cantankerous hoddydoddy." He said he invented these phrases by "brain doodling."*

Dreams of the Sea

William, or Bill, Steig was born on November 14, 1907. He lived in Brooklyn, New York. Bill's family later moved to the Bronx neighborhood of New York City. His father, Joseph, was a housepainter. His mother, Laura, was a **seamstress**.

Joseph and Laura were **immigrants** from Lemberg, which is now part of the Ukraine. Bill had three brothers. Irwin and Henry were older than Bill. Arthur was his younger brother.

The Steig family was very artistic. Joseph painted postcards on weekends. Laura and Irwin painted, too. In fact, Irwin gave Bill his first painting lesson. Bill's parents encouraged their children's interest in art.

Joseph and Laura were **Socialists**. They believed their children would be taken advantage of if they worked for someone else. They also thought it would be wrong if their children owned a business and hired other people. They felt their kids would do best working for themselves. Being an artist was one way to do that.

Bill was not sure he wanted to be an artist, however. He grew up dreaming of being a sailor or a beach bum. He especially wanted to go to Tahiti. He definitely did not want a regular job.

The Steigs were a family of artists. Their artwork was exhibited in a show called "The Eight Performing Steigs, Artists All," at a New York gallery in 1945.

Family Breadwinner

Bill began showing his artwork in his high school newspaper. He preferred drawing or playing sports to studying, however. He later admitted that he did not get much of his education there. He graduated from high school when he was just 15!

After graduation, Bill spent two years at the City College of New York. He then spent three years at the National Academy of Design. Once, he even tried the Yale School of Fine Arts. He dropped out after just five days. Bill still dreamed of going to sea and wandering.

A painting by Steig of his mother

The **Great Depression** put a stop to Bill's daydreams. Joseph had invested much of the family's money in the **stock market**. He lost it when the stock market crashed in 1929. Joseph and Laura looked to Bill for help. So, he had to get a job.

At this time, Bill was 23 years old. The only thing he thought he could do was draw. So, he began drawing cartoons and showing them to magazines. By June 1930, Bill was selling cartoons to the *New Yorker*. He earned about $4,500 his first year. In 1930, that was enough to support his family.

Within a couple of years, many people were seeing Bill's work. Several of his cartoons appeared in a book of collected art called *The Stag at Eve*. In 1932, he published his own collection called *Man About Town*. Most of the cartoons in the book had appeared in the *New Yorker*.

Steig also created wood carvings and exhibited them at an art gallery.

Popular Artist

Most of Steig's works were funny cartoons. In the mid-1930s, he started working on a new kind of drawing. Steig described different types of people with these cartoons. He called them symbolic drawings.

The editors at the *New Yorker* were not interested in the drawings at first. So, Steig published them in his own books. Steig's career as an artist was now in full swing.

By this time, Steig had met a young woman named Elizabeth Mead. He and Liza, as he called her, married in January 1936. Steig's earnings allowed them to move into a nice apartment in New York City. They had a daughter, Lucy, in 1940. They had a son, Jeremy, in 1942.

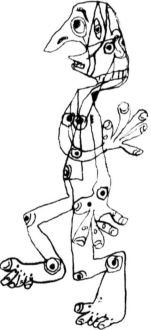

One of Steig's symbolic sketches

During the next 20 years, Steig created more illustrations and books for adults. Steig also illustrated advertisements in the 1960s. However, he hated it. He believed art should be for enjoyment, not for selling things. So in 1968, he started down a new road. It led to writing and drawing for children.

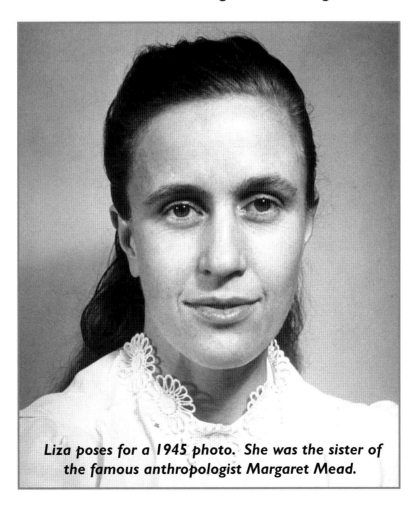

Liza poses for a 1945 photo. She was the sister of the famous anthropologist Margaret Mead.

CDB! and the Donkey

Steig was nearly 60 years old when a friend asked him to do a book for children. The friend's name was Robert Kraus. Kraus was setting up a new company that would publish children's books.

Steig did not need much convincing. He got to work right away. He realized he had many ideas for children's books. In many ways, he still thought just like a child.

His first book was *CDB!*. The title sounds like "see the bee." In fact, the whole book's text is nothing but single letters that sound like words. The letters and drawings tell the story.

Steig published *CDB!* in 1968. He published a second book that same year. It was called *Roland the Minstrel Pig.* Roland is a pig who loves playing the lute and singing.

A lute is a stringed instrument. It would be very difficult for a pig to play!

While writing children's books, Steig continued drawing for the New Yorker. He was the magazine's longest-running contributor with 71 years of artwork, including 121 covers and more than 1,600 drawings.

Steig began sending other stories to Kraus. One of them was about Sylvester the donkey. *Sylvester and the Magic Pebble* tells how Sylvester accidentally turns himself into a rock. The rest of the story is about his parents' search for him.

Once the story was accepted, Steig's next task was figuring out the drawings. Steig had to decide whether Sylvester should walk on two legs or four. Plus, he had to show how sad Sylvester's parents were when they lost their son.

Steig's own life may have influenced his story. By this time, he and Liza had divorced. Steig had remarried and had a daughter, Maggie, with his new wife. After his second divorce, Maggie left Steig to live with her mother. So, Steig could understand how Sylvester's parents felt upon losing their child.

Steig's sketches show his interesting use of shape.

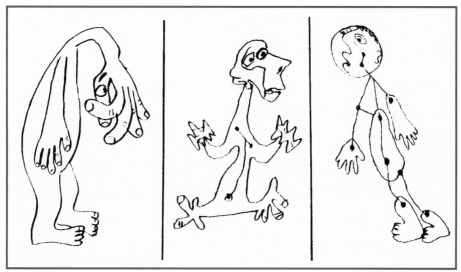

Shape

Elements of Art

Shape is one of the basic parts of art. Shapes are formed when lines come together. They can be geometric like circles, squares, and triangles. They can also be irregular and squiggly. These types of shapes are called organic. Artists often begin sketches with just basic shapes.

Illustrators have to make many decisions about the shapes in their pictures. William Steig spent a lot of time thinking about the shapes in *Sylvester and the Magic Pebble*. He thought about the rock that Sylvester becomes. He considered shaping the rock like a donkey. He ended up making it more like a normal rock.

More Success

Sylvester and the Magic Pebble was published in 1969. It won the **Caldecott Medal**. Steig was very happy. Not everyone loved the book, however.

In the story, Sylvester's parents seek help from the police. The police are drawn as pigs, which offended some people. Steig explained that he thought pigs were good symbols for people. Plus, he just liked drawing pigs.

Steig's next books also featured animals. He filled the pages of *The Bad Island* with all kinds of brightly colored, ill-behaved creatures. Eventually, a single flower helps change the island. *The Bad Island* was published in 1969. It became one of Steig's favorite books.

Steig followed *The Bad Island* with *An Eye for Elephant*, *The Bad Speller*, and *Amos & Boris*. *Amos & Boris* is about the friendship between a mouse and a whale.

Amos & Boris was Steig's first book with a new publisher called Farrar, Straus & Giroux. The editor there encouraged Steig to consider writing longer stories for children. He took the editor's advice and produced *Dominic*, *The Real Thief*, and *Abel's Island. Abel's Island* received a **Newbery Honor**.

The Caldecott Medal is named after Randolph Caldecott. He was an artist who illustrated children's books in the late 1800s.

Creating Colorful Characters

Steig continued to produce picture books and wrote *The Amazing Bone* in 1976. It tells the story of Pearl, a pig who finds a magical bone. *The Amazing Bone* was named a **Caldecott Honor Book**.

Steig's next book was his first to feature major human characters. *Caleb & Kate* is about the relationship between a carpenter and a weaver. The book explores how people can like each other but still annoy one another, too.

In 1982, Steig created one of his most popular books. *Doctor De Soto* is about a mouse who is a dentist. The dentist must find a way to treat a fox's tooth without becoming the fox's next meal. The book received a 1983 **Newbery Honor**. Steig wrote a **sequel** in 1992 called *Doctor De Soto Goes to Africa*.

In 1990, Steig created another very popular character in a book called *Shrek!*. Shrek is an ogre who looks bad, smells bad, and enjoys every minute of it. He manages to find a perfect mate with the help of a witch. The two then "live horribly ever after."

Shrek! was made into a movie in 2001. *Shrek* won an **Academy Award** in the **animated** feature film category. A **sequel** to the movie was released in May 2004.

After divorcing his third wife in 1964, Steig married his fourth wife in 1969. They began working together on projects in the 1980s. Jeanne Steig wrote the verses for **Consider the Lemming,** *published in 1988. The pair also created* **The Old Testament Made Easy** *in 1990 and* **Alpha Beta Chowder** *in 1992.*

Final Chapters

By the 1990s, Steig had been writing children's books for more than 20 years. He also continued to draw cartoons and illustrations for adults. He brought both of these skills together in a book for adults and kids in 1995. He called it *Grown-Ups Get to Do All the Driving.*

Steig worked closely with his editors on his later books. Once, he and his editor spent a long day working on a story. Both agreed it was not very good. However, they needed a book to present to the publisher. They had to start from scratch.

Finally, the editor asked Steig if he ever played any special games with his kids. Steig said he sometimes pretended to turn his daughter Maggie into a pizza. This idea led to *Pete's a Pizza.* In it, Pete's father rolls him and tosses him like dough. The book was published in 1998.

Steig's final book was about his own childhood. It was called *When Everybody Wore a Hat.* The book talks about Steig's life growing up in The Bronx.

In **When Everybody Wore a Hat,** *Steig remembered his parents, Joseph and Laura.*

William Steig died on October 3, 2003, in Boston, Massachusetts. He was 95 years old. His books were very popular during his lifetime. And, his work continues to entertain children and adults today.

Glossary

Academy Award - an award given by the Academy of Motion Picture Arts and Sciences to the best actors and filmmakers of the year.

animation - a process involving a series of pictures or drawings that appear to move.

Caldecott Medal - an award the American Library Association gives to the artist who illustrated the year's best picture book. Runners-up are called Caldecott Honor Books.

Great Depression - a period (from 1929 to 1942) of worldwide economic trouble when there was little buying or selling, and many people could not find work.

immigration - entry into another country to live. A person who immigrates is called an immigrant.

Newbery Medal - an award the American Library Association gives to the author who writes the year's best book for young readers. Runners-up are called Newbery Honor Books.

seamstress - a woman who sews clothes.

sequel - a book or movie continuing a story that began previously.

socialism - a kind of economy in which either the government or all of the citizens control the production and distribution of goods. A person who believes in socialism is called a Socialist.

stock market - a place where stocks and bonds, which represent parts of businesses, are bought and sold.

Web Sites

To learn more about William Steig, visit ABDO Publishing Company on the World Wide Web at **www.abdopub.com**. Web sites about William Steig are featured on our Book Links page. These links are routinely monitored and updated to provide the most current information available.

Index

A
Abel's Island 17
Amazing Bone, The 18
Amos & Boris 16, 17

B
Bad Island, The 16
Bad Speller, The 16
Boston, Massachusetts 21
Bronx 6, 20
Brooklyn, New York 6

C
Caldecott Honor Book 18
Caldecott Medal 16
Caleb & Kate 18
CDB! 12
City College of New York 8

D
Doctor De Soto 4, 18
Doctor De Soto Goes to Africa 18
Dominic 17

E
Eye for Elephant, An 16

F
family 6, 8, 9, 10, 14, 20
Farrar, Straus & Giroux 17

G
Great Depression 8
Grown-Ups Get to Do All the Driving 20

K
Kraus, Robert 12, 14

L
Lemberg 6

M
Man About Town 9

N
National Academy of Design 8
New York City, New York 6, 10
New Yorker 4, 9, 10
Newbery Honor 17

P
Pete's a Pizza 20

R
Real Thief, The 17
Roland the Minstrel Pig 12

S
Shrek! (book) 4, 18, 19
Shrek (movie) 19
Stag at Eve, The 9
Sylvester and the Magic Pebble 4, 14, 16
symbolic drawings 10

U
Ukraine 6

W
When Everybody Wore a Hat 20

Y
Yale School of Fine Arts 8